against identity

against

LEON WIESELTIER

identity

WILLIAM DRENTTEL NEW YORK 1996

A shorter version of *Against Identity* was originally published in *The New Republic*.

ISBN 1 884381 11 1 *cloth*
ISBN 1 884381 12 X *paper*

171 Duane Street New York New York 10013

For Martin Peretz

I

We call ourselves what we are, but also what we wish to be. This is inspiring and this is corrupting. For the ambiguity allows us to see the one in the other, to mistake what we wish to be for what we are. Since the satisfaction of an ideal is so hard to attain, it is so easy to imagine. But the reality of an ideal must not blind us to its unreality, which is the source of its incitement to action, and of its usefulness as a measure of progress. A good rule is: we are never already what we should be.

2

Every culture has its preferred description of the human distinction. These descriptions are analytical and homiletical. In our civilization, they have included: the soul, the nous (and other appellations for the mind), the self, the ego, the person. In our time, the preferred description is: identity. In America, and not only in America, we are choking on identity. And not only on the identity of others; we are choking also on the identity of our own. What if the disgruntlement of America is owed to something deeper than social and political schemes of preferment? What if we are presenting ourselves to each other, and to ourselves, in a manner that simplifies, and distorts, and diminishes? What if we are promoting a coarse and troublesome description?

3

"I seize the word *identity*," wrote Robert Penn Warren in 1965. "It is a key word. You hear it over and over again." A few years earlier there appeared a book that described the United States as *The Identity Society*. Identity, according to Erik Erikson, writing in the 1950s, is "vague," "ambiguous," "unfathomable," "colloquial," "naive," "all-pervasive." Identity was certainly one of the most repercussive contributions of the social sciences to American culture. But what was it? For social scientistic intellectuals in postwar America, identity was what alienation was not. It was the promise of home. For Erikson, it was a slogan for the end of childhood, for the crucible of adolescence, for the success of socialization. (The crucible of adolescence: there is an example of Eriksonian sentimentality.) Finally Erkison's influence on the American obsession with identity was less a theory than a mood. He made identity into a romance.

4

The idea of identity originates in logic. A=A. This is an assertion of sameness and an assertion of difference. An object is the same as all the objects that are like itself and it is different from all the objects that are not like itself. Now consider an analogy between the logical relation and the social relation. A=A. The question, *What is your identity?* is really the question, *Who are you like?* Identity, in other words, is a euphemism for conformity. It announces a desire to be subsumed, an eagerness to be known primarily by a common characteristic. I say primarily, since identity need not be perfect to be absolute. Logicians talk of "identity in difference." Objects that are the same with respect to one criterion of identity may be different with respect to another criterion of identity. And it is never the case, even with simple objects, that there is a single criterion of identity. The ascription of identity, then, is the consequence of a choice among the criteria of identity. We have many likenesses, but we do not reward them all with significance.

5

A=A. This is also a way of saying that A≠B. Which might bruise B. There is solace, of course. It is that B=B. But this is also a way of saying that B≠A. Which might bruise A. Identity is very social, but it is not very sociable.

6

The definition of the individual known as "identity" is not least a negative definition, a definition not only of what one is, but also of what one is not; and such a definition of the same will often be experienced by the other as a rejection. Identity is an insulation; a doctrine of aversion; an exaltation of impassability. The bad news (and the good news) is that the insulation is never adequate. The borders are permeable, and strange gods slip across.

7

The cracks in identity let democracy through. Whatever the philosophical premise of democracy, the existential premise of democracy is this: somebody like and unlike myself is already here with me.

Identity is not to be mistaken for individuality. Individuality is ancient, identity is modern. In his last lecture, in 1938, Marcel Mauss observed: "It is plain that there has never existed a human being who has not been aware, not only of his body, but also at the same time of his individuality, both spiritual and physical." It is more plausible to think of identity as the solution to the problem of individuality.

9

It is never long before identity is reduced to loyalty.

10

An affiliation is not an experience. It is, in fact, a surrogate for experience. Identity is the articulation of this surrogacy. Where the faith in God is wanting, there is still religious identity. Where the bed is cold and empty, there is still sexual identity. Where the words of the fathers are forgotten, there is still ethnic identity. The thinner the identity, the louder.

II

Pride has a happy use for ignorance.

12

The hardest thing in America is to be what one is softly.

13

Private identity is an oxymoron. Identity is public, it is how one is known. Secret identity, by contrast, is entirely possible. It is not a reflection of inward realities, but of outward realities. Secret identity is a stratagem for survival, the characteristic improvisation of a minority in danger. It has a long and strenuous past. The history of the Jews is replete with instances of desperate and dignified self-concealment, most famously in fifteenth-century Spain, and so is the history of homosexuality. (For all the African American anxiety about "passing," it is one of the defining hardships of this minority that its identity cannot be hidden.)

14

Identity in bad times is not like identity in good times. The vigorous expression of identity in the face of oppression is not an exercise of narcissism, it is an exercise of heroism. And those qualities of identity that seem vexing and impoverishing in good times—the soldierliness and the obsession with solidarity, the renunciation of individual development in the name of collective development, the reliance on symbolic action, the belief in the cruelty of the world and the eternity of struggle—are precisely the qualities that provide the social and psychological foundations for resistance. For this reason, it is impertinent to address the criticism of identity to those whose existence is threatened. Still, justice sometimes comes. And when it comes, it is bewildering, because it proposes peace to selves that have been arranged for war. The identity that changed history yesterday is redundant today. The outer discontinuity demands an inner discontinuity, which is wrenching. Unless a rupture of identity is accomplished, there will be justice, but there will not be peace.

15

Identity is too eager to commemorate itself. It is nourished by its nightmare, by possibility of its extinction.

16

Who are you? Even when you know the answer, it is not an easy question.

17

The spell of identity is not difficult to comprehend. Hume's horror, we might call our situation. With his pained discussion of personal identity, Hume ended his quest for "the uninterrupted and invariable object." He failed to find it. He found instead that "the mind is a kind of theatre.... Our eyes cannot turn in their sockets without varying our perceptions. Our thought is still more variable than our sight; and all our other senses and faculties contribute to this change; nor is there any single power of the soul which remains unalterably the same." There was nothing steady, nothing firm, nothing solid; only associations and patterns of associations. Hume's pages were written in a tone of affable despair. And this was two centuries before our bacchanal of associations! The stimulations have never been faster or fiercer than they are today. The technology of information from which we prosper, and from which we suffer, makes the clutter that troubled Hume look like order, and his mind's theater look like a place of repose. We are unprecedentedly distracted and unprecedentedly dispersed. Hume took some comfort from the operation of memory, which confers a sense of continuity; but memory in the modern world is disappearing beneath the assault of associations. We are carrying too much. We are falling out of our hands. We need a basket. The name of the basket is identity.

18

We have a craving for specificity, but we love also to slip away from specificity. We want to be one thing, but not any longer this one thing or that one thing. We have a fear of being nothing and a fantasy of being everything, but we do not see that everything is a busy version of nothing. So one cheer for identity: it imposes discipline. It is the enemy of "the protean self."

19

A proponent of "the protean self" praises it for its "radical fluidity, functional wisdom, and a quest for at least minimal form," which is the appropriate response to "the flux of our time." "The protean self," says Robert Jay Lifton, is characterized by "serial equipoise" and "rolling configurations." It "can transcend time and space—to contain simultaneously elements from highly divergent historical periods and equally divergent geographical and cultural places. The protean self need not be just here or there but can be here *and* there..." And so on. Lifton is right that the self is resilient; but surely resilience is the antithesis of malleability. To change is to survive, but it is not to resist. And "here *and* there" is not quite so easy. There is a difference between living doubly and living promiscuously. The "protean self" is the promiscuous self, the suave and shallow self, the self that adopts the standpoint of the consumer as an ideal of life, the self for which tragedy is a variety of stress, the self that stands in dread of silence. Lifton has provided the psychology of post-modernism. But Proteus, remember, was not resilient, he was slippery. He had an objective in transforming himself into a lion and a serpent and a boar and a tree, and it was not the cultivation of his personality. He assumed his many shapes in order to escape Menelaos's questions. He was, in sum, a dodger: a fine post-modern god of the sea. Identity, at least, is prepared to take questions.

20

The old upbuilding discourse: purity of heart is to will one thing. The new upbuilding discourse: purity of heart is to will one thing at a time.

21

Every inheritance is an accident. This is what religious, sexual, and ethnic identity is designed to make one forget. For a feeling of contingency, it substitutes a feeling of necessity. But it is not necessary to be necessary, if one is prepared to work. There is no shame in being accidental. I am not ashamed that I might not have been a man or a Jew. Indeed, the awareness that I might not have been a man or a Jew prepares me with a patience for the many things that I might have been. A feeling of contingency is a useful impediment to vanity. Anyway, it is possible to be proud of one's luck: not as one is proud of what one has made, but as one is proud of what one has understood.

22

Identity is toasty. It imparts a feeling of the inside; but this feeling is imparted to us from the outside. The inside, the outside: they must be properly mapped. The country to which I belong is outside, the people to which I belong is outside, the family to which I belong is outside. Inside, there is only my body and my soul. From the beginning, I recognize this family as my family and this people as my people and this country as my country; but not in the way that I recognize this body as my body and this soul as my soul. I am not estranged from my family and my people and my country, but neither are we the same. I must bring them from the outside in, if I am to love them for more than circumstance. And circumstance is a poor reason for love. And the inside is vast, too.

23

Identity thrives on facts: you are the child of this man and this woman, this neighborhood, this town, this nation, this faith, this country. But there is one fact to which identity is oblivious, and that is the fact of individuation: you are nobody else and nobody else is you. There is no sharper experience of facticity than the experience of individuation, from which the only relief is sleep.

24

It is not fair to attack the group for failing to banish loneliness. But it is also not fair for the group to promise that it will banish loneliness.

25

Kierkegaard said that it is easier for somebody who is not a Christian to become a Christian than it is for somebody who is a Christian to become a Christian. I am always at a disadvantage toward my own tradition. I am not only quickened by my intimacy with what I have been given, I am also dulled by it. I lack the wakefulness of the stranger. I should conduct myself toward the tradition to which I have fallen heir like an actor who has played a scene poorly: I should go out and come in again.

26

It is possible to suffer from the opposite of homesickness. This is more than sickness of home. It is a desire to concentrate oneself without references, to vibrate in a featureless environment, entirely out of one's own powers, with an energy that owes nothing to the energy of origins. There is such a longing.

27

To know about a thing that it is yours is to know little about it.

28

There is the excitement of discovering one's own, but there is also the excitement of discovering one's difference with one's own. The study of medieval Hebrew texts taught me this. So many of them were so profoundly unfamiliar to me. I experienced the shock of a lack of recognition. This was a Jewish universe not known to me. In order to understand many of these peculiar, vivacious, turgid, and irresistible documents, I had to learn to imagine Jews. I acquired this skill by leaving my "Jewish identity" at the door of the seminar room. For it is an axiom of that identity that a Jew is a Jew is a Jew; but the study of Jewish history showed that this axiom was a necessary fiction. We were not only one thing, we were also many things. The complication was delicious. Here was diversity, but on the inside. As a boy, I had been taught that it was my duty to choose Jewishness, and I have always warmed to the choice; but I was thrilled to understand that it was my duty also to choose among Jewishnesses. This made the tradition stir, and secured it against a museological petrifaction. And so I set out to gain the knowledge that would be required for the judgment of my own patrimonies. A few years later, in the same room on the top floor of the library, I read this sentence in a story by Hawthorne: "Let us thank God for having given us such ancestors; and let each successive generation thank him, not less fervently, for being one step further from them in the march of ages."

29

It is a special delight to find oneself alone with one's own tradition. There are forgotten corners to which one escapes without escaping; ideas or texts or images that are rarely visited by the others; tranquil peripheries where the contradiction between privacy and participation, between solitude and solidarity, disappears. A secret room under the same roof.

30

It is important to distinguish between identifying oneself and justifying oneself. Identity in America is so fitful and so flexible not least because it is often cobbled together for the purpose of self-justification; and this constant clamor for self-justification is a drain on American dignity. One must defend oneself, of course, if one is attacked for being a black or a homosexual or a woman or a Jew or a Catholic, but one must aspire to be more than a defender of oneself. To assert your right to be something is not yet to be something.

31

The lure of identity is the lure of wholeness. It proposes to bind up the parts and the pieces of a life and transform them into a unity, into a life that adds up. This provides a mixture of psychological and aesthetic elation. But is there really nothing worse than a life that does not add up? Surely the life that adds up is the easeful one. Erikson was right to remark that "an increasing sense of identity... is experienced as a sense of psychosocial well-being," but he was making a damning admission.

32

The thirst for wholeness is indistinguishable from the thirst for death. Only religion is candid enough to say so.

33

In the modern world, the cruelest thing you can do to people is to make them ashamed of their complexity.

34

A life that does not add up is not a life of irony. Quite the contrary. Its accomplishment is to contain within itself many things that do not go together, all of them unironically. Irony used to have an aspect of courage, in a time when inconsistency was an occasion for pain. But no longer. This is a time when inconsistency is an occasion for pleasure. (The name of that pleasure is post-modernism.) And so the quality of courage is to be sought in literalness, in taking words and ideas and things for what they are and following them far.

35

Two cheers for identity: it is the enemy of irony.

36

I hear it said of somebody that he is leading a double life.
I think to myself: Just two?

37

"A double minded man is unstable in all his ways.... Purify your hearts, ye double minded." St. James was a realist about the mind. He saw that the mind will not surrender its multiplicity, and so it requires the intervention of the heart. But he was not a realist about the heart. The heart, too, chases many things.

38

In America, the tribunes of identity are the tribunes of diversity, but the joke is on them. Their ends are contradictory. Diversity means complexity. Identity means simplicity. Anybody who takes diversity seriously will see that identity is an illusion. The multiculturalists will reply that there is no contradiction, that America is a complex society of differently simplified individuals, a multicultural society of monocultural people. But they misunderstand America. The American accomplishment is not the multicultural society, it is the multicultural individual. And the multicultural individual is what the tribalists and the traditionalists (they are not always the same people) fear. Identity is a promise of singleness, but this is a false promise. Many things are possible in America, but the singleness of identity is not one of them.

39

Self-reliance is no longer possible when the work of one's hands is viewed as the seizure of what one is owed.

Pluralism is hard, for individuals and for groups. In the United States, we have been so dazzled by our pluralism that we have forgotten its hardships. Pluralism, after all, is premised not only on difference, but also on the proximity of difference: another way to live is almost never out of mind in America, because it is almost never out of sight. The sidewalks are crowded with incommensurabilities. You live and work and play with people for whom your worldview is nonsense, or worse. Exclusiveness is an illusion, where experience is porous. When everything is everywhere, there is no safety in numbers. There is safety only in sameness; and so pluralism frequently provokes convulsions of sameness. The movement in culture and politics known as multiculturalism is one of those convulsions. It will pass, but it will come again. It is a regular feature of the American situation. Multiculturalism claims to originate in a fear of homogeneity, of an erasure of the particular by the general; but in truth it reflects a fear of heterogeneity, which is a classically American fear.

41

Not: my identity, but: my identities. There is a greater truth in the plural. There is also a greater likelihood of decency. The multicultural individual is a figure of moral friction. In such an individual the mocker, and the hater, and the killer, may hit a bump.

42

For Erikson, "identity formation begins where the usefulness of multiple identification ends." But the usefulness of multiple identification never ends.

43

The absence of coherence is not yet incoherence.

On what grounds does one accept one's identity? If the grounds are internal, then one's identity is weak. If the grounds are external, then one's identity is strong—but then there is a principle in the world stronger than identity, to which we must all appeal.

45

The fervor with which a proposition is believed tells nothing about its truth. Except for its practical consequences, passion is beside the point.

The multiculturalists are Herder's children. (The Afrocentrists especially.) They have created a cult of incommensurability. But if the differences between individuals and groups were as thick and as final as the multiculturalists think, then not even multiculturalism would be possible. Everybody, the one and the many, would be shut up in subjectivity. There would be only total silence or total war.

47

I will praise what makes us different if you will praise what makes us the same. We must not all praise the one or the other, or we will be stranded between the insignificance of a tribe and the insignificance of a species.

48

Misunderstanding, prejudice, conflict: they are all twisted tributes to the possibility of objectivity. They occur on, and mar, a common ground. That is why they can be refuted or resolved.

49

From our everyday experience of generalization, we draw the conclusion that the particular is prior to the general. This is a mistake. The general is prior to the particular. Our differences are versions of our similarities.

50

Human beings have roots, but they are not plants.

51

The secret of universalism is that it works.

52

If I cannot explain myself to people who are not like me, I lose my pleasure in explaining myself to people who are like me.

53

There is no point in leading others to what you cherish, if you believe that they cannot follow you. Pride in one's difference makes no sense if differences are blinding, if others cannot see.

54

"The reason why all water is said to be specifically the same as all other water is because of a certain likeness it bears to it, and the only difference in the case of water drawn from the same spring is this, that the likeness is more emphatic." This, from Aristotle's discussion of sameness in the *Topics*. What a beautiful formulation of tolerance, for the universal and the particular. Unfortunately, you cannot make a politics out of a metaphor.

55

Authenticity is a paltry standard by which to appraise an idea or a work of art or a political position. Authenticity is a measure of provenance, and provenance has nothing to do with substance. An idea may be ours and still be false. A work of art may be ours and still be ugly. A political position may be ours and still be evil.

56

Authenticity is a reactionary ideal. Speaking strictly, it is an anti-ideal. It says: what has been is what must be. It is the idolatry of origins.

57

A = A. Big deal.

58

In the discussion of multiculturalism, there has been a good deal of indignation about the relativism among traditions; but there is also the relativism within traditions. The latter is a consequence of multiculturalism that has not been sufficiently noted. When an expression is judged for its authenticity, distinctions of value within a tradition collapse. I have observed this in the American Jewish community, where food and philosophy are promoted almost in the same spirit, since they are both Jewish expressions, and so they fill the same need. Not in the same individuals, of course, but in the same group, which (for this sort of thinking) is what counts. But Maimonides is not like a bowl of soup. Maimonides is one of the most powerful minds in the history of human thought. Those Jews who kindle to *The Guide of the Perplexed* because it is the work of a Jew are not wrong, but they are impoverished. They rob themselves of the exquisite satisfaction of coming upon something of universal importance in one's own midst.

59

I sit in my room, a white man, and listen to *East St. Louis Toodle-oo* and *Lull at Dawn* and *Cotton Tail* and *Blood Count.* I am certain that I do not hear these pieces the way a black man hears them. But I am also certain that I hear them rightly, since I hear them as music. If you prize Ellington for the reason that he was a black man, you do not have to listen to him. You would prize him just as ardently if you were deaf.

"I love it because it is mine." This is the language of identity. Properly translated, this means: I do not love it, I love me.

61

You can change your religion but you cannot change your grandfather, said a nineteenth-century German Jewish liberal, who changed his religion. This pronouncement is cheap, in the way that identity can be cheap. It expects the fathers to do the work of the sons. This man betrayed his grandfather and then counted on his grandfather to save him from disgrace. But the finality of one's origins should not secure one against the accountability of one's actions. Also, it should be harder to change your religion than your grandfather.

It is a part of the glamour of identity that it is received. Otherwise one could not enjoy the sensation of being a link in the chain of transmission. But this passivity is a conceit, and an expression of indolence. Traditions are not only given, they are also made. In recent years historians have written a great deal about "the invention of tradition," some of them a little too breathlessly. It is not exactly news that people put things into their past and then claim that they found them there. Still, the historians have a point. Identity relies heavily on the receptive attitude, but it is not the receptive attitude by which traditions grow. A tradition that is transmitted more or less as it is received will not live long.

63

A tradition is a field of intentions and exertions. It has not been given merely because it has been received, and it has not been received merely because it has been given.

64

"Rabbi Yose said: Make yourself fit for the study of Torah, for it is not an inheritance." Not an inheritance: this, from the first century in Judea, gives the problem of tradition, the illusion of tradition, in all its brutality. A thousand years later, in the eleventh century in France, the passage was glossed: "And do not say that since my father was a scholar, I, too, will be a scholar, without toiling and straining." I come upon this anxiety in the grandest Talmudic culture in the history of the Jewish diaspora and I squirm. They thought that they were not carrying their own weight! So for centuries we have been warned. The biological does not establish the spiritual. Like the sins of the fathers, the illuminations of the fathers will not be visited upon the sons.

65

What is made should be celebrated as much as what is given, not least because it is made out of what is given.

66

Perhaps identity is a kind of realism about human affairs. It is preferable, certainly, to the preposterous Nietzscheanism according to which we must, as we brush our teeth in the morning, start all over again and devise the foundations of our world. Who, really, is such a hero? (Not Richard Rorty.) And yet this is an unacceptable choice. The world is not completely stable and it is not completely unstable. The same is true of the self. The uninflected life of identity asks too little, but the inflection of identity is not an insignificant thing. It should be honored. Adding a little is harder than taking away a lot. And a blessing on the souls who begin at the beginning.

67

Identity is a fixative, and it works on the elements of a life the way a fixative works on the elements of a drawing: it holds them together and it helps them to withstand the light.

68

Erikson drew a distinction between the notion of wholeness and the notion of totality. "To say it in one sentence: when the human being, because of accidental or developmental shifts, loses an essential wholeness, he restructures himself and the world by taking recourse to what we may call totalism." This was written in 1954, when the analysis of totalitarianism was in full swing. Identity, in Erikson's view, allowed for the realization of "a much-desired wholeness," whereas totalitarianism was the inhibitor of identity, for which it substituted regressive formations of totality. From the standpoint of politics, however, Erikson's distinction between wholeness and totality is trivial. Seek wholeness and you will likely find totality. The hunger for wholeness always plays into the hands of the hunger for totality. The monsters of modern history, in other words, had a use for identity. Before the identity politics of the 1980s and 1990s, there was the identity politics of the 1930s and 1940s. Now, and for a long time to come, Sarajevo is the capital of this continuity. The city teaches that the relationship between identity and morality may be a crushing one.

69

Wholeness is unreflective, but totality is clever.

70

Identity will always look suspiciously on selflessness. But selflessness does not mean that you do not have yourself or that you do not know yourself. It means that you have been drawn out of yourself. It is the self-denial of the strong.

71

I will not find the true or the good or the beautiful because I hate myself, but it helps. When I repel myself, I am no longer at rest. My discontent is a kind of propulsion, a centrifugal motion of the soul.

72

Purity is the opposite of integrity.

—I feel like jumping out of my skin.
—And so you should.

Only one in possession of an identity would understand why one would wish to be rid of it.

colophon

A shorter collection of these aphorisms first appeared in *The New Republic* in 1995. They are published here in a limited edition of 100 copies. A separate edition has also been issued in wrappers. The text is set in Spectrum, a typeface designed by Jan Van Krimpen in 1943. Designed by Jessica Helfand and William Drenttel, this book was imaged from a Macintosh file by Michael Josefowicz of Red Ink Productions in New York City, and bound by the Campbell Logan Bindery in Minneapolis.